# THE HIDDEN SEASON

# THE HIDDEN SEASON

by
JAMIE D. MITCHELL

THE HIDDEN SEASON

© 2013 by Jamie D. Mitchell

ISBN 978-0-98968-560-3

Unless otherwise noted, all Scripture quotations are taken from the King James Version of the Bible.

All scripture quotations, unless otherwise indicated, are taken from the HOLY BIBLE, NEW INTERNATIONAL VERSION ®. NIV®. Copyright © 1973, 1978, 1984 by International Bible Society. Used by permission of Zondervan Publishing House. All rights reserved.

Printed in the United States of America by Create Space.

*In Loving Memory of*

…my grandmother Annie Mae Shoffner and my dear friend Bishop Reginald Kelly who always lent a listening ear and kind words of encouragement.

You are truly missed.

*Dedication*

I would like to dedicate this book to every person in life who feels like they have not accomplished their dreams and to those who feel like they have been overlooked by others. You have not been overlooked. God has you hidden for a reason and a season.

*Acknowledgements*

My heartfelt appreciation goes to my family and friends for their encouragement and love.

I would like to thank my mother, Alma and my sisters Shirley, Carolyn, Linda, Teresa, Brenda and a special thanks to my niece Tiffany, my nephew Michael, cousin Termell and best friend Bishop Cheryl Grissom.

# CONTENTS

# INTRODUCTION

## TO EVERYTHING THERE IS A SEASON AND A TIME TO EVERY PURPOSE UNDER THE HEAVEN: ECCLESIATES 3:1

There are various seasons in our lives when we go through certain things. The Word of God was written to instruct and encourage us and to let us know that life will get better. All the test and trials we go through are for a reason. Sometimes God has us in "hiding" for our making and He is perfecting the part of us that needs to be perfected. *"The Lord will fulfill his purpose for me; your love, O Lord, endures forever— do not abandon the works of your hands (Psalm 138:8 NIV)."* When we come forth we will be like Him.

The Hidden Season is a book of inspirational poetry relating to seasons that will take place in the believer's life. During the seasons we are being made to be all God has called and wants us to be. I pray this book will be an encouragement to the body of Christ and keep you lifted in the Spirit. May it remind you that if you see yourself in any of these seasons, God your Deliverer is going to bring you out. Wait on the Lord and let Him do what He wants to do-through you and in you. *"But they that wait upon the Lord shall renew their strength; they shall mount up with wings as eagles; they shall run, and not be weary; and they shall walk and not faint (Isaiah 40:31 KJV)."*

*You, O Lord, keep my lamp burning;*

*my God turns my darkness into light.*

*Psalm 18:28 (NIV)*

# THAT HOUR OF DARKNESS

I can't begin to imagine what Jesus went through
In His hour of darkness,
I wouldn't have known what to do
At times we have an hour of darkness in our lives
Wondering when things are going to be alright

Sometimes this hour
Seems like years
We have to keep looking up
And hold back the tears

In your hour of darkness
You may feel like you have been forsaken
But tell the enemy he is a liar
And he is mistaken

Even though many things happen
In this dark hour
There is something you must remember
Jesus our Savior has all power

In this hour
Sometimes you may feel like asking
God "are you there?"
Just know that Jesus can comfort you
He really does care

In your dark hour, you may say to yourself
"When are my blessings going to take place?
How many more trials and tests
What more do I have to face?"

But just hold on
Sometimes your hour is not as long as you think
Daybreak is coming
You are right at the brink

At the end of your dark hour
Things begin to turn
This is when you realize
You did learn

Out of everything you went through
All of your trials and your tests
You had to go this route
So others could be blessed

You can now share with others
Your hour of darkness doesn't look so dark
All you have to do is be patient
Wait and trust in God

*Cast all your anxiety on him because he*

*cares for you.*

*1 Peter 5:7 (NIV)*

# DON'T GIVE UP

Sometimes in life
You may want to give up
But you must believe
And keep looking up

Lift up your head
O ye gates
Don't give up now
It is not too late

You may say "I've waited on the Lord
And it has been a long time"
Trust God He will see you through
And you will be just fine

He is never too busy
He has a listening ear
He's always willing
And ready to hear

Cast your cares upon Him
He cares for you
He understands
He knows what to do

He wants you to trust Him
All of your days
So acknowledge Him
In all of your ways

He will give you divine direction
On the right way to go
Just follow His leading
He will let you know

You must seek the Lord
He won't let you go wrong
If you seem to be weak
He will make you strong

Trust in the Lord
As His word declares you should
No matter what happens
God is still good

Through the storms in life
Whatever they may be
Stand on God's Word
You already have the victory

*But thanks be to God!  He gives us the victory through our Lord Jesus Christ.*

1 Corinthians 15:57 (NIV)

# VICTR'Y SHOES

I have these old shoes
I sometimes put on my feet
They put a tingle in me
That makes me jump and leap

It's like VICTR'Y takes over
Whenever I wear these shoes
They make me so joyful and peaceful
I can't even hear bad news

These shoes carry my feet
To a place of endurance
I call them VICTR'Y shoes
Because they bring deliverance

I remember King David in the Bible
And how he had to fight
He thought on the goodness of God
And danced before the Lord with all his might

VICTR'Y was sho nuff in his shoes
And had to be in his feet
He knew the power of praise
And the challenges he had to meet

One thing about these kind of shoes
They keep you lifted up everyday
They let you know Christ has already given you the
VICTR'Y
Even when you pray

I hope you have a pair of these shoes
You can shout the VICTR'Y in
One thing about this kind of VICTR'Y
Christ fixed it so we would win

*The end of a matter is better than its beginning, and patience is better than pride.*

*Ecclesiastes 7:8 (NIV)*

# THE WINTER SEASON

As snow falls
Soft and white
Your day will get better
Also your night

Snow melts sometimes
Before it hits the ground
So do problems when given to Jesus
Because He is always around

This is the winter season
And things seem cold
This is the season
You must be bold

With winter you don't know
Exactly what to expect
It may be snowing one day
And sunshine the very next

Although you may have
Some terrible ice storms
Jesus is there
And He will keep you calm

Sometimes an ice storm
Makes you panic and scared
But keep the faith
Because Jesus really does care

In your winter season
You don't have to worry
Jesus will be there
In a hurry

The winter season
Doesn't last too long
It comes quick
And then it is gone

Jesus promises your winter season
Will soon come to an end
And you will be
Peaceful and joyful again

Your next season
Will be so much better than your last
What you have asked God for
Will come to pass

*For in the day of trouble he will keep me safe in his dwelling; he will hide me in the shelter of his tabernacle and set me high upon a rock.*

Psalm 27:5 (NIV)

# THE HIDDEN SEASON

Perhaps you are going through
Rough and trying times
You hardly seem to have
Any peace of mind

You have been persecuted
And wondering why
Maybe sometimes
You have had to cry

You might feel like you are going nowhere
And life has done you wrong
But God is wanting
You to be strong

"Look at my servant Moses
In the Word
Have you read about him
Or have you heard

I had him in hiding
When he was a child
He was hid
For just a short while

I placed him in Pharaoh's house
For a reason
I knew I would bring him forth
In due season

Moses was in training
Learning some skills
I knew I could use him
To do My will

I knew I had to keep him hid
In that hour
Because when he came forth
He would be miraculous with power

He could not come forth
Before his time
If he would have
It could have messed up his mind

There was something in Moses
I wanted to use
I wanted to show him
He was not born to lose

So if you feel like
You have not come forth like you should
God himself
Wants to offer something good

If you are not being heard
There is a reason
God has you in hiding
For this season

He wants you
To learn all about Him
So when you come forth
You will be just like Him

Maybe you feel like
You have been lost in the process
But God is perfecting you
To be one of his best

God has to get rid
Of the flesh man's skills
So you can only
Do His will

When you get to the point
It is no longer, the I,
But the Christ in me
The you, will have died and the world will see

God has done
What He wanted to do
That it is only Him
And no longer you

Now it is your turn
And God has His reason
You are no longer
In the hidden season

People will be blessed
Saved and made free
They can get delivered
And be what God called them to be

Spending time with God
Has many good reasons
You will see things looking better
Because it is your season

To be anointed
And used by God
People will see
Life is not hard

All that you went through
Was for a reason
It is God's appointed time for you
Because it is your season

*But he knows the way that I take;*

*when he has tested me, I will come*

*forth as gold.*

*Job 23:10 (NIV)*

# THE JOB SEASON

No one knows
What you go through
You can't tell anyone
Because they will just look at you

You've had to go
Behind the closed door
And cry it out
Even more

At this time
You are wondering, where is God?
People have been laughing at you
Real hard

Asking you
Where is the God you serve?
If you were living right
He would have heard

The enemy makes you start thinking
God they are right
I've served you a long time
Almost all of my life

You must not entertain
Those bad thoughts
Jesus has already paid the price
And you've been bought

I say to you go to the Word
And look at Job
He was a man
Who was tried like gold

He was tested and tried
One trial after another
He did not look
To a sister or brother

Job could not
Look to his wife
She wanted him to curse God and die
And give up on life

Job acknowledged who God is
And he knew he would win
He blessed God out of his mouth
And he did not sin

God knew
He could brag on this man
Job would bless him
Even if he did not understand

Although Job
Was really put to the test
In the end
He was doubly blessed

Hold on
No matter how long it takes
All of your blessings
Will be worth the wait

God is saying, "I've called you at this time
To be all you can be
You are made in My image and My likeness
And you look just like Me"

*I will exalt you, my God the King; I will*

*praise your name for ever and ever.*

*Psalm 145:1 (NIV)*

# PRAISERS

Lift up your head
Oh ye praisers of Judah
God has made you
A leader and a ruler

God wants you to praise Him
Because there is power in praise
Don't just stand there
And be in a daze

Put on your garment of praise
Every day you live
You are a praiser
And you were born to give

To give all the praise
That He is due
It does not matter
What you go through

All things are working together
For your good
So praise God
Like you know you should

In everything give thanks
Whatever it might be
Always be honest
And keep your integrity

Don't just praise God
Worship Him too
You'll find yourself
Being refreshed and renewed

Worship the Lord
With holy reverence
I guarantee you
You will usher in his presence

When the enemy comes
And you are all alone
Just ask yourself
Do you have your garment of praise on?

*I will praise the Lord, who counsels me;*

*even at night my heart instructs me.*

*Psalm 16:7 (NIV)*

# THE NIGHT SEASON

Can you feel the breeze
Of the night wind
Blowing swiftly and softly
Upon your chin

You are walking outside
In the night air
Wondering
If anyone cares

In the night season
Sometimes things look a little dim
But God lets you know
You can trust in Him

In this season
You look forward to day
Telling yourself
It has got to be a better way

You may be wondering
When will daybreak come?
Asking God
Where is Jesus his son?

All of a sudden you hear a still small voice
Talking to you in your ear
Yes, you are ready
To listen and hear

There's a whisper that is inspiring
From God above
He reaches in your ear to tell you
You are loved

Then you look up
And see a ray of light
Something so beautiful
And yes it is bright

God talks to you
For a little while
Things look good
As you start to smile

It is morning now
And joy came
Lifetime looks better and does not
Look the same

The night is gone
And daybreak is here
Jesus let me know
I don't have to fear

He also told me
I can trust Him at all times
Because I am His
And He is mine

*A cheerful heart is good medicine, but a crushed spirit dries up the bones.*

*Proverbs 17:22 (NIV)*

# LAUGH

I woke up this morning
And the telephone was disconnected
This was the day
I felt I had been elected

To be picked on by the enemy
To see what I would do
So I began to laugh
Because I knew God would see me through

I went outside to get in the car
As I looked from afar
What to my surprise did I see
A flat tire staring at me

I began to laugh at the enemy
Even more now
I knew I had to keep my joy
Anyhow

I knew the enemy
Was after my joy this day
I laughed and laughed
Because I knew what to say

Bless the Lord, bless the Lord
I thought to myself
I know God
Is still my help

All of the bills
Were overdue and late
But I knew these trials
Was a test of my fate

On my way to work
I laughed even harder
When I thought about the flat tire
To begin my day as a starter

I thought about how things
Hit you in life
I smiled even more
Because I knew it would be all right

I couldn't get depressed
Because I didn't have any money
I had to laugh
Because it was so funny

I understood the enemy
Was after my joy
And if I let him
He would use it like a toy

I know this joy
Did not come from the world
Man cannot give it to you
Neither man, woman, boy, nor girl

So on tomorrow
At the start of the day
Rejoice in the Lord and I say
Rejoice all the way

*Heal me, O LORD, and I will be healed;*
*save me and I will be saved, for you are*
*the one I praise.*

*Jeremiah 17:14 (NIV)*

# THE HEALING SEASON

Maybe you had to cry in this season
And it brought lots of rain
Troubles that happened to you
Brought different types of pain

Perhaps someone hurt you real bad
And you couldn't see
You started to question and ask God
Why is this happening to me?

Maybe there was a pain where someone lied
And you began to hurt
Maybe they looked down on you
And treated you like dirt

Then there was the pain of death
Where a family member or someone you loved passed
You had been so close to them you began to wonder
How long will this pain last?

Maybe there was the pain of where sickness came
And you had no feelings
But all of a sudden you began to pray
And a miracle stepped in called healing

At first you thought about how you were hurting
And how this pain seemed so real
You cried out and confessed to God
I am hurting and I need to be healed

Then you felt the burdens being removed
And lifting with ease
Everything you were feeling was no longer there
And the pain began to leave

You grasp now you must always pray
No matter how hard the trial
Prayer changes life's situations for you
And leaves you with a smile

Just knowing who God is
And who He is to you
You understand now He was there all the time
Even when you went through

When pain tries to come and upset you
And wants you to hurt again
Just speak to pain and say "be thou gone
You are not my friend"

Like an eagle you can mount up
And now soar through the air
You don't have to hurt anymore
Because Jesus has all your care

*but those who hope in the LORD will renew their strength. They will soar on wings like eagles; they will run and not grow weary, they will walk and not be faint.*

*Isaiah 40:31 (NIV)*

# IT'S MY TIME

It is not time
For us to sit down
And hang our head down
With a frown

It's time for us to get up
And get what is rightfully ours
Because we are living
In this last hour

It's time for us
To do all we can
To get up
And possess our land

It's time for us
To take back everything the devil stole
We should be in tune
Like the prophets of old

They walked and talked
And stayed in tune with God
They had a relationship
From the heart

Miracles took place
And it did not take long
To show them God was powerful
Mighty and strong

Don't look
At what you are going through
It's a setup for God
To work a miracle for you

You might be saying
I have been through this before
But in God's appointed time
He will open every door

It's time for us
To trust God and believe
Then your miracles can take place
And you can receive

We can't have the up today
And down tomorrow syndrome
And when things are not working out
We say everything is wrong

Get up and praise God
In the midst of your going through
If you notice when you praise God
He works miracles for you

Don't listen to the enemy
Telling you his lies and mess
Turn around and say "devil you are a liar
And it's my time to be blessed

I will wait on the Lord
And I can go to any length
I am like an eagle
Because I have the strength

To mount up with wings
Because it's my time and people will see
I am going to get my miracle
And everything else God has for me

*Rejoice in the Lord always.  I will say it again: Rejoice!*

*Philippians 4:4 (NIV)*

# HALLELUJAH PLACE

I've traveled down this road before
And things still look the same
Maybe there was something that I missed
Because I was looking for a change

I remembered the obstacles in my way
And how I reacted in the past
I said maybe this time I can make a difference
And things won't seem so bad

I didn't stop on the corner of Bad Attitude Drive
Neither did I yield
I remembered this time
I wanted to be in the Lord's will

The last time that I went this route
I got a little impatient and upset
This was something I didn't want to go through again
Because I didn't know everything just yet

This time I stopped at Praise Boulevard
Where everything was good and royal
I went down one block
And there was a sign called joyful

I saw a balloon fly up in the air
And say you should not complain
As I looked up I ran into Hallelujah place
And the sign had written on it, Hallelujah in Jesus name

Everywhere I turned down this street
Signs were lit up and I was amazed
Every street told you to lift Jesus up
And every sign dealt with praise

I decided to build me a house
Along this street
All of a sudden I began to dance before the Lord
And it felt like fire in my feet

Some more saints saw me praising God
And said "Lord what's wrong with her?"
She's jumping and shouting so hard
I don't think she has a care

All of the people got excited
And they came over to this house
Everything that had breath was praising God
And they began to shout

They said joy is truly on this street
And God truly is here
We just want to thank you Lord
For filling us with cheer

They began to thank God for this joy
And how he is so wonderful and kind
They thanked God for allowing Hallelujah place to be
built
And they told him it was built just in time

So when the enemy tries to get you depressed
And make you cry and tear up your face
Just tell the enemy, no not this time
I'm going to Hallelujah place

*It is a good thing to give thanks unto the LORD, and to sing praises unto thy name, O most High:*

*Psalm 92:1 (KJV)*

# THE WHEN WILL SEASON

When will life get better
It has been several years
I have cried many days
And shed many tears

When will I get to the point in life
I am tired of struggling and being in debt
When will all of my bills get paid
And all of my needs get met

When will I reach my goals in life
I have set so many
When will I accomplish my businesses
I said I would have plenty

When will I wake up
And realize what I have is good
When will I recognize
It is okay to be misunderstood

When will I look at life
And see life is great
When will I get a grip
And learn how to relate

One day I looked at life
And I thanked God for what I had
Everything that has happened to me
Has not been all bad

I realized I should value God's blessings
And thank Him for every one
Stop complaining about what I don't have
And see the great things God has done

Trust in the LORD with all your heart
and lean not on your own
understanding; in all your ways
acknowledge him, and he will make
your paths straight.

Proverbs 3:5-6 (NIV)

# THE OPEN DOOR SEASON

God has opened a door
He opened it especially for you
All you have to do is look up
And just walk right on through

Don't let people stop you
From pursuing what you want to acquire
You can go on and seek your dream
And fulfill your heart's desire

God opens doors no man can shut
No matter what people have said
When it is your turn for God
To pour out his blessings on you
You want be the tail but you will be the head

When this door opens
Don't wait on anyone else
You want to hear the voice of God
Even if you have to encourage yourself

You have the favor of God
Pray for Him to direct your path
You will need His help
All you have to do is ask

You have been waiting for this moment
And your life's dream has been on your mind
Your day has finally come
Now it is your time

*I WILL bless the LORD at all times: his praise shall continually be in my mouth.*

*Psalms 34:1 (KJV)*

# THE ENCOURAGEMENT SEASON

There is a season in your life
Sometimes you may get depressed
This is the season you may have to comprehend
God made you one of his best

He knew this day would come
And you would feel very low
But He is standing there
To let you know

He loves you
Although you may not understand
Just look up to Him
He is there to hold your hand

This is a season
You may not feel like you have anything left
This is the season
You have to encourage yourself

Remember if God brought you out of situations
And carried you through
Stand on His promises
Because the Word of God is true

*A man's gift maketh room for him, and bringeth him before great men.*

*Proverbs 18:16 (KJV)*

# SEEDS OF GREATNESS

God has put greatness in someone special like you
And He planted the seed
You don't have to worry
Because He will supply all of your need

God has planted a seed
On the inside of you
It is called greatness
Because He chose you

God has given you dreams
That you want to fulfill
Seek His face
And find out His will

God has put greatness in you
Don't settle for second best
You must pursue your dreams
And get in the press

Be determined to use the gift of greatness
That is why God planted the seed in you
He knew you could accomplish
Everything you set your mind to do

Whatever your dream is
That you have in your heart
Give it everything you've got
The seed of greatness comes from God

*The Lord is good to those whose hope is in him, to the one who seeks him;*

Lamentations 3:25

# WHAT HAPPENS AT DAYBREAK

What happens at daybreak
Joy comes in the morning
There is a new day
And a new dawning

What happens at daybreak
I can finally see the light
I am much stronger now
Because my future looks bright

What happens at daybreak
Things are going my way
I see God moving
It is a new day

What happens at daybreak
A change takes place
No more struggles
Do I have to face

What happens at daybreak
I must pray to God and believe
I must have faith
In order to succeed

I went through some storms
During the night
I saw God in the midst
And now everything is alright

When daybreak came
I finally understood
I tasted and I saw
That the Lord is good

*And let us not be weary in well doing:*

*for in due season we shall reap, if we*

*faint not.*

Galatians 6:9 (KJV)

# THE 3 FACES OF CHANGE

Sometimes you get tired of going around in circles
And wondering what to do
You have to believe and keep praying
That God will see you through

You cannot sit around
And wait on others when it is time for a change
You have got to get up and make things happen
And go on in Jesus name

You may have been thinking
When is my change going to come
I have wasted time
Things should have already been done

You may have had
A lot of things on your mind
It is not too late to get started
You are not behind time

Don't look at your season as being too late
You can move forward right now
It is not as bad as it looks
You have got to go on with change anyhow

God has put a gift in you
It is up to you to work your gift
If you need an extra boost
Pray and God will give you a lift

The 1st face you need for change
Is to pray and seek the face of God
When you put Him first
You will realize change is not hard

The 2nd thing you need to face
Is to trust in the Lord to direct your path
For that change that you need
All you have to do is ask

Change comes with making a decision
What you should have done a long time ago
Maybe you procrastinated a long time
And you kept moving slow

Sometimes you have to do things yourself
In order for things to take place
You will have obstacles and challenges
Some things you will have to face

The 3rd thing you need to face is to believe God
He will give you everything you need
It is time for you to make a move
He made you to succeed

# PRAYER FOR SALVATION

If you do not know the Lord Jesus Christ as your personal savior, you can get to know Him on today.

*That if thou shalt confess with thy mouth the Lord Jesus, and shalt believe in thine heart God hath raised him from the dead, thou shalt be saved. For with the heart man believeth unto righteousness; and with the mouth confession is made unto salvation.*

*Romans 10:9-10 (KJV)*

Father, I ask that you come into my heart and cleanse me from all my sins. I do confess with my mouth and I do believe in my heart God hath raised Jesus from the dead and I thank you I am saved. Father fill me with your spirit in Jesus name.

# Words of Encouragement

Some of us as Christians in the body of Christ may sometimes sit and wonder when is my time or change going to come. Sometimes we feel like we have confessed the Word and having done all we know to do but it looks like nothing is changing or going to happen. One thing about God is that if He said it in His Word, it's already settled in heaven.

God is so awesome. When we think all hope is gone because we have been waiting for a long time, He steps in and does exactly what He said He would do. We as Christians need to let God be God in our lives and quit trying to fix our situations ourselves. Just know that you have a due season that God brings you out of hiding.

You don't have to sit and tell yourself anymore, this is not the will of God for my life. In all walks of life you will be persecuted or lied on, talked about or misunderstood. This is all a part of your process of being in your Hidden Season. Through this book I pray you have been encouraged.

# About the Author

Jamie Mitchell is a writer and a poet. She attended North Carolina Agricultural and Technical State University and is a graduate of Guilford Technical Community College.

She is a licensed Minister and an ordained Deaconess. At the age of twenty-two, she accepted the Lord Jesus Christ as her personal Savior. Over the years, Jamie served as a Sunday School Teacher, a Youth Pastor, and taught a Faith Builders class. Jamie loves the Lord with all her heart and loves seeing lives transformed by the Word of God. She is a teacher of the Gospel of Jesus Christ.

Poetry has been a passion of Jamie's for many years. She has been inspired to write for family and friends. Some of her most memorable poems include "Don't Give Up," and "The Hidden Season." Jamie Mitchell resides in Greensboro, North Carolina.